The Art of Dying

Other Works by Red Hawk

Journey of the Medicine Man
   (August House)

The Sioux Dog Dance
   (Cleveland State University Press)

The Way of Power
   (Hohm Press)

The Art of Dying

Poems by Red Hawk
(Hawk Fecit)
Work or Die.

HOHM PRESS
PRESCOTT, AZ

Acknowledgments
Some of these poems have appeared in the following
journals:
   TAWAGOTO: *Today You Must Slap Me; The King of the
   World.*
   THE SUN: *The Namer; They Leave You Here Alone in
   the Dark; The Day I Beat My Father.*
   VIHA CONNECTION: *For Vedan, Who Died Young.*
   RAISING ISSUES: *The Last Time I Hit My Daughter.*
   ATLANTA REVIEW: *2 Ways of Crossing the Creek.*
   BLACK WARRIOR REVIEW: *Sometimes Things Don't
   Add Up.*
   KENYON REVIEW: *2 Ways of Crossing the Creek.*
   CAROLINA REVIEW: *TV One.*

Cover Design and Art: "Fate's Way" by Gary Simmons
(133 Brown Dr., Hot Springs, Ark. 71913)
Title Page Art: Joe Hodges (Red Dot), (P.O. Box 250394,
Little Rock, Ark. 72225-0394
Layout: Universal Graphics, Danville, California and
Shukyo Lin Rainey, San Rafael, California

Library of Congress Cataloging in Publication Data:
Red Hawk.
   The art of dying : poems / by Red Hawk.
          p.   cm.
   ISBN 0-934252-93-9 (alk. paper)
   I. Title.
PS3568.E295A89   1999
811'.54--dc21
                                    99-25118
                                      CIP

HOHM PRESS
P.O. Box 2501
Prescott, AZ 86302
800-381-2700
http://www.hohmpress.com

Printed in U.S.A. on recycled, acid-free
paper using soy ink.

DEDICATION

This book is for Little Wind and Rain Drop;
   For Osho, Mister Lee,
     Yogi Ramsuratkumar;
   For Chandrika, Worthy Companion;
   For Tommy Logan, Sandy Irwin,
     and Joy Richardson;
   For Mary Louise and Bill Irwin:
     The Guardians.

CONTENTS

PROLOGUE: The Art of Dying
    The Art of Dying................................. xiii

PART I: Death Like a Dirty Dog
    London Texas, 1937 1
    The Keepers of the Bones 2
    How the Apache Made You Talk 3
    TV One 4
    How I Envy the Success of Other Poets 5
    What Happens When You Get Everything
        You Want..................................... 6
    The Bureaucratic Mind 7
    The Cost of Killing the Animals 8
    The Problem With Human Intelligence.......... 9
    Wolf 10
    Sometimes Things Don't Add Up 11
    They Leave You Here Alone in the Dark 12
    Easy 13
    She Worshipped the Bottle 14
    Religion 15
    How Easy It is to Forget God 17
    How Love Dies 18
    The Day I Beat My Father 19
    The Day My Father Died 20
    One More for Sonny 21
    Did My Father Thrill to See Me?...... 22
    My Grandmother's Letters 23
    30 Geese on the Lawn 25
    Getting Famous 26

PART II: Death By Surrender

The Way is Within 29
The House of a Strong Woman 30
The Stonecutter and the Potter 31
4 Beautiful Women Approaching Darkness 32
The Fragrance of My Love is Like a Flower
    (for Chandrika) 33
The Power of Longing 34
Shunyata: Emptiness is Your Friend
    (for Little Bear) 35
The King of the World 36
In Praise of the Man of Faith 38
Why I Am Not Famous 40
Mister Lee and the Art of Flower Arranging..... 41
Jesus Lives in Arizona 42
Purna's Teaching 43
Naboni's Smoking Mixture 44
Today You Must Slap Me 46
The Argument for Whipping Our Children
    (for Monty Roberts) 47
The Last Time I Hit My Daughter 49
Humbled By Love 50
My Daughter's First Smile 51
The Placental Broth 52
The Gift of the Parents 54
The Impossible Elegance of Power 55
Robert E. Lee in Richmond 57
Jimmy Driftwood's Guitar (for BR) 58
Mike Disfarmer, Shadow-Seer 59
2 Ways of Crossing the Creek 61
The Digger of Shallow Wells
    (Shallow Well Project: 618-997-5365) 63
How the Drought Behaves................................. 65
The Long Legged Heron in the Water 67
The Beautiful Poem Written By A Tree............ 69

PART III: Death By Attention

For Vedan, Who Died Young 73
Voluntary Simplicity 74
The Law of Karma 76
The Boy Jesus in the Wood Shop 78
God is in the Details 79
The Good Farmer 80
Spiritual Practice is Not Complicated 82
Mosquito Hawk.. 83
The Arrowsmith Woman 84
The Medicine Stone 86
The Courage of Sitting Bull 88
Sitting Bull's Revenge 90
Sitting Bull's Horse (for Little Bear) 91
Grass Dancer 93
The Namer 95
After the Poetry Reading 96
Some Meditations on the Art of Poetry 97
"Poems Should Be Written Rarely
    and Reluctantly (. . . Czeslaw Milosz) 99
How Rare to Find Honor Among the Artists 100
Miller Williams Delivers the Inaugural Poem 101
Politics 102
2 Breeds of Cat.. 103
What It Takes 104
Nothing Left 105
The Condemned Man 106
Zero the Swine Clerk... 107
Zero the Feed Mill Clerk 108
For Tom, Whose Baby Died............................... 109
Little Wind Learns to Speak.............................. 111

EPILOGUE:
We Practice All Our Lives for a Single Moment
   We Practice All Our Lives
   for a Single Moment 115

About The Author 116

PROLOGUE
The Art of Dying

The Art of Dying

The task is to maintain correct behavior
in the face of the unknown,
in the face of the terror of the mind:
to relax into the darkness of the body
riding a smile   repeating
        God.   ohh God.
Dance out quietly on the last wave
of breath
where death waits for you
grinning.

Pay no attention to him;
do not be fooled by his disguises.
He may look like your mother
but he is just the boatman
across the river of Light.
Let him dance and sing,
let him go on grinning,
let him call to you
        son.   darling.

Watch the center of the Light.
Do not look away for anything.
You must begin your practice now.
I know the boatman;
he will do what you wish.
The task is to maintain correct behavior:
smile   relax   watch closely;
let the boatman row you away.

PART I
Death Like a Dirty Dog

London Texas, 1937

It was an oil rich boom town
stuck right in the middle of the
East Texas field, one of the
biggest and richest oil finds
ever discovered. The local school board

was rolling in dough, but
like the rest of us they still
thought like cheap losers so
just to save a few bucks and
avoid paying for fuel oil

for their school furnace, they tapped into
an oil company gas pipeline illegally
to heat the school. A cloud of natural gas
built up in the basement and on March 18,
1937, just before the final bell

to send the children home, a spark
lifted the school off its concrete pad
like a clumsy, stumbling rocket ship
and sent the roof flying into the sky.
It landed on the bodies of 293 dead and

gave the term 'boom town' a new meaning.
The town killed its children and then it died.
The heartbroken people moved away.
A year later the town council
held a memorial service for the dead children

and no one ever came.
Once the children have been killed
it leaves a void which can't be filled
with anything but shame.
Upon this soil the damned Souls build.

The Keepers of the Bones

To understand the white man's mind
you need look no further than the Smithsonian,
in the basement where the air is
cooled and the humidity carefully controlled.

That is where they keep the bones of the Indians,
thousands of them.
One section, half a block long, is just skulls.
They have examined the bones closely,

sectioned them under electron microscopes,
carbon-dated, analyzed and dissected them,
weighed and measured them,
catalogued, cross-referenced and stored them,

put it all down in books, every ounce and
scrap in boxes lining the wooden cases row
upon terrible row and when the tribes ask
them to return the bones for proper disposal

they refuse. They say
these belong to the Federal Government,
and they believe it.
In all their books it does not say

what they were looking for or
if they ever found it.
Once a reporter asked Sitting Bull
why the Indians didn't bury their dead.

The crows and the worms,
all the scavengers have to eat too;
what good is the body to us
once the Spirit has left it,

he said. It belongs
to the Earth, not
to us, he said and they
took his picture for the paper.

How the Apache Made You Talk

They staked you down naked
in the dust, in the Sun
with a piece of wet rawhide wrapped
tight around your head and that
staked down too so you could not
turn your head right or left

and then

they put a small borer-worm
in your ear
and as the wet rawhide dried and tightened
and the worm bored in
no matter how brave and tough you were,
you babbled helplessly,

you spoke every single secret thing

and an old Apache woman sat nearby
under a lone tree or the shade
of a Mesquite bush and she listened and
when she heard what she was after
she cut your throat. The Apache after all
were not mindlessly cruel, but frugal:

they did what was needed, no more.

TV One

In every classroom it clicks on
all by itself and then
when it is done with what it
has to say it
clicks itself off.

When it comes on,
first there is the news and
none of the children watch.
They babble, they fight, they
curse their lives. But

when the commercials come on

all eyes turn.
There is no talk.
If one of them speaks
the others shoosh him.

Fashion is what they
kill for. This
is what they are being
trained and set up for,

to consume without question
as they are being consumed.

How I Envy the Success
of Other Poets

Every poet in the country who wins a prize,
gets a big grant or a good position, I despise
because I wish it were otherwise:

me honored, he dies.

What Happens When You Get
Everything You Want

Alice was married to the richest man in town
and for years she lived a life of luxury:
anything she wanted he got for her and
she wanted a lot.
Then Eddie moved to town
and she wanted him too, but
that was the one thing her husband
didn't go for, so she left him and she
married Eddie.
He wore a pink satin robe around the house,
meditated in the living room and
never had a job, just lived
off her divorce settlement.
Then in 2 months she left him so
I had to ask her why.
At first she wouldn't tell.
I can't, she'd say, I'm too ashamed.
That made me burn; I tried to imagine
what sexual atrocities he demanded of her but,
No, that wasn't it, she said so then
one day she told me: Every night
when he got in bed, Eddie
blew his nose on my sheets, she said
and she began to weep.
Some men just can't stand success.
Take Eddie for instance;
he had it made
but he blew it.

The Bureaucratic Mind

In Utah they still shoot condemned men.
They used to sit them
tied to a high-backed wooden chair
but they noticed the chair back
was getting shot full of holes
and they had to buy new chairs so
they figured out they could
sit the criminal on a bench.
Then they figured out that if
they only put live rounds in 2

of the firing squad's guns
they would save money that way
and if they pinned a
little white target
over the condemned person's heart
they were less likely to
waste either of the 2 good rounds.
The bureaucratic mind works slow
but if you give it enough time,
the way the Nazi's did,

it can solve any problem.

The Cost of Killing the Animals

If the Earth is a vital body, then
organic life is its organ system,
trees its lungs, water its blood,
like that.

Each organ gives off a unique force
crucial to the life of the body.
If one organ dies,
another must take over its function

or the Earth dies.
We are killing off the animals, so
humans must assume their function
which means massive numbers of us

must live like dogs, only
without a dog's devotion,
lacking a dog's courage.
We must live lives of simple brutality

and constant sexual tension.
We must reproduce in vast numbers
to replace the slaughtered animals.
We must pay

by becoming them,
living like lizards,
dying like dogs.
That is the Law and

we are bound to it
the way a dog
is bound by a chain
to a tree.

The Problem With Human Intelligence

Easter Island is a remarkable place
not only for its giant stone statues,
one thousand of them, each weighing
18 tons and standing 15 feet tall, but

also for its fossil pollen record and
what it tells us about Human Beings.
Easter Island is completely treeless
but the fossil pollen tells us that

a fruit palm tree flourished on Easter Island
for thousands of years and the decline of that species
began about 1200 years ago and continued for
several hundred years until the tree became extinct.

1200 years ago is when the Humans came to Easter Island.
If you stand on the island's highest point
you can see nearly the entire island so
the people knew what they were doing:

systematically they were destroying their paradise
and the man who cut the last tree, the very thing
he depended upon for his survival,
knew it was the last tree standing and

he cut it anyway.

Wolf

Wolf was half Shepherd, half wolf,
one of those good dogs who
suffered from an excess of courage
and too few brains,

like so many I have known.
One day we were in a rowboat
on Lake Ouachita, early morning,
water calm and smooth like

the air around the dying
and I rowed into the rushes
to get a close look at a beaver dam.
We saw them at the same time,

4 of them, big ones swimming near us
but Wolf was quicker than my lunge
and over the side before I could stop him.
I thought, My God he'll kill them, but

that is not the way it worked.
They were smart, they
went under and took his legs
right off

so he screamed and drowned
before I could get a paddle on them.
Courage is more common than you think;
many have it, but very few

manage it in such a way that
it is a virtue.

Sometimes Things Don't Add Up

Me and Bill Buclair sit in the back row,
flunking algebra and taking the japes and jeers
of the others in the class who are glad
we are there because it means that
no matter how bad things get for them
they are not the dumbest of the lot.
But one day both our parents get a call.
It is the algebra teacher. He says that
unless we pass the next test me and Buclair
will fail the course.
We study like hell for a week and
when the teacher gives back the tests he says,
There are only 2 perfect scores in the class,
then he gives the papers to me and Buclair
to hand out.
After that we sit in the back of the class,
still goofing off and giggling, take our D
for the course, but nobody gives us any more shit.
It shook them.
Something terrible had happened
in the back of the room,
what they had all figured out
turned on them and
no longer added up:
if me and Buclair could be perfect,
the world as they knew it
was in flames. Suddenly
there was no net under them
and they were out there all alone
on a shaky rope, me and Buclair
at either end,
knives in our hands.

They Leave You Here Alone in the Dark

When I was 4 years old they put me in the hospital
to remove my tonsils and adnoids.
The night after they operated
I could not sleep so I got up

and I wandered down the huge corridor,
nobody in sight and I came to 2 big doors
so I went through them and that is when
I first heard the sound of real pain;

I had wandered into the children's burn unit
and everywhere like a black tornado cloud
rolling above the treeline
there were the dark sobs and moans,

a terrifying noise in the bones and cells,
the emanations of illiterate flesh.
Next to where I stood dumbstruck
was a boy whose arms were bandaged but

otherwise he was okay. You
shouldn't be here, he whispered so
I moved over next to him, our eyes
reaching for one another in the dark.

What happened to you, I asked him
trying not to cry.
Don't play with matches, he said,
it hurts real bad and

they leave you here alone in the dark.
I was only 4. I could not bear
that much truth: when he said 'they'
I thought he meant the matches.

Easy

She was good to me
when I was a boy and in desperate need
of some goodness.
She is very rich, charters private jets
to get to her Florida condo on the beach.
When I tell this to someone they say,
Man she's got it easy.

I do not tell how
she takes the oxygen tank with her
everywhere she goes so she can
get a breath, her whole life reduced
to the next breath;
how along with the emphysema she has
chronic bronchitis so every time she laughs

the phlegm rises in her tortured lungs
and she strangles as she coughs;
how her back is humped and twisted
so she walks bent double with a walker;
how she was once the most beautiful woman
I had ever seen and now
all of it has been taken from her.

No one has it easy here;
we all walk alone
in the hell
of our own devising
but I do not say it.
Yeah, I say, she's
got it easy.

She Worshipped the Bottle

I have known some women
who loved the bottle, but
I've never seen another
like my mother.
Every day she went to her
secret hiding holes,
pulled out the cheap wine and
drank it down until she fell over,
laid there half the day, got up
and did it all over again.
And when the holes were dry, she
drank vanilla extract, Geritol,
cough medicine, Aqua Velva aftershave,
shoe polish and rubbing alcohol,
anything, anything at all
to feed the demon
that had stolen her heart.
I have seldom seen such love again,
such great capacity for giving.
She was a saint my mother,
a voyager in the dream, a meditator.
When the dawn bell pealed
in the empty sky,
she went to her knees
in a revery of devotion,
brought forth her sacraments,
drank her bitter cup
in penance for her sorrows,
fell down before her Master
and remained there
until she died, having
given everything she had
for her faith.

Religion

Barbara Bishop was the first girl
I ever loved and you could make a case
that I have never loved another
half so well.

Black hair, dark eyes, precariously, exquisitely
balanced on the fine line between full bodied and plump,
thick soft full warm wet beautiful shapely lips,
she was the finest kiss I have ever known and

we could not wait for Friday night when
we got in the car and went hell bent for anywhere
anywhere
so we could kiss each other with all the

tongue and lip and tooth and mouth and spit
that it is possible for 2 humans to exchange until
the steam was so thick on the windows that
it rolled in fleshy rivers down the slickened glass.

Both virgins, that is all we ever did
and it was better than any sex I have ever known
and holier than any religion
and then we stopped because she was

catholic and guilty about it
and the one true religious ecstasy
of both our lives
got shut off like a hot water faucet.

There are some who say religion has
done a lot of good
for the general level of humanity
but I do not see it and

I do not care at all
for the way it has
frightened hot wet steamy delicious
young girls into being nice.

How Easy It is to Forget God

Once when Logan was a boy in Africa
he climbed a sheer cliff, rocks and river
beneath, clear sky above, almost nothing
to hold on to. 10 feet from the top
he gets to a place where there is nothing
to hold on to. He cannot go down,
he cannot go up, so for 30 minutes
he holds on in a cold soak,

peeing a drop at a time and praying
that if God saves him just this once
he will never do anything so stupid again.
Just out of reach above him Logan sees
what looks like a hand hold, but he
has to let go and jump to get it.
If it is a hold, he's saved. If it
isn't, he's gone on the rocks below.

He jumps.

It is.
So he gets to the top, down the other side,
back to the river and there is a beautiful girl
in the Sun on top of the rocks.
I just climbed that cliff, Logan says.
No you didn't, she laughs at him.
Oh yeah, he says,
Watch this.

How Love Dies

It is brought down by my lies.
Not the large ones I use to save my place
in the world, but the small ones I sift
through conscience to save my delicate face.
How I justify and compromise,
how easily I trample the gift
of Love, slay it to avoid the disgrace
of being exposed as empty, adrift
in the fragile lie of self, pretending to be wise.

Love is humble and it is swift
to yield to deceit. A lie carves
up the Heart and Love's soft cries
go unheard. Once Love dies
the Heart dries up
and the Soul starves.
Lie by lie I am degraded;
I grow jaded to Love.
My deceit consumes me without a trace.

The Day I Beat My Father

After Mother died
it was over between us, we
rarely spoke to one another in that
house owned by death, and

when we did speak it was
in the language of wolves,
a snarl and a curse, a brief flash
of fang in passing.

But one night just before I left for good
it all came to its inevitable clash.
Drunk as always he swung at me
as always, but things had changed

for me. I didn't take it as always.
I blocked it with one arm easily,
grabbed him by the throat, bent him
over the dining room table, drew back

ready to pay off on all the beatings,
the cruel mindless drunken rages, the
humiliations of my mother and sister,
all of it boiling in my fist but then

I saw him, old and cowering, mad
and far gone, lost in the forest like me, weak
and hopeless. I dropped it right there
and walked away, never looked back again.

You may long for it, dream of it,
pray for the day that it comes but
it is never any good
when you beat your old man.

The Day My Father Died

When a tyrant dies
the people dance in the streets and
for a few minutes, maybe even a day
or two they are no longer afraid.

So when they brought me the news
in the house where I lived at school
that my father was dead
I did what anyone would have done,

I danced.
This scared the boys I lived with, they
were not used to one of their number
showing any kind of honest feeling

but all I could think of was the years
of beatings and curses and vile bullying
and so when they came in with the news
as we were all seated at the dinner table,

I said, Good!
and I jumped up clapping my hands
and did a little jig, I was so relieved to hear it.
Soon after that they threw me out

and they mentioned before they voted that
how I took this news was not normal.
They could not tolerate
one for whom his father's death

held no weeping; they had no sense
of history so they did not know
that when a tyrant dies,
the people dance in the streets.

One More for Sonny

He was a momma's boy a long time
before he was my father. She
called him Sonny but he
did not shine.

He was a dandy, liked narrow shoes,
silk socks and ties,
but when he bought a suit for me, his excuse
for getting it in too large a size

was that it gave me room to grow.
His mother was an overbearing witch
who adored her only Sonny so,
it made him a selfish son-of-a-bitch.

If the Son is the center of her universe,
then the mother's love becomes a curse;
too much unrelieved cherishing
makes a hard road between birth and perishing.

Did My Father Thrill to See Me?

My daughters melted my heart
and made a cruel man kind.
Light poured from their faces into that part
of me which was withered, cold, blind

and numb with sorrows. With unfettered ease
they performed daily miracles, restoring me to life.
Now I wonder at my own dead father: did it please
his tortured heart to look on me, or was the knife

of his self-hatred sharper than my joy
at loving him; did his heart leap as mine
does now, when I crawled into his arms, a small boy
full of adoration; did his face shine

briefly, did his grief melt in momentary wonder
before the storm of madness raged him with its thunder?

My Grandmother's Letters

She wrote letters to all the world's great leaders
telling them in a calm, reasonable voice
just where they had gone wrong
and what they should do about it.

The one to Hitler went:
Dear Mister Hitler,
You must stop killing the Jews.
I have known many Jewish people

and they were all fine and decent.
I wonder what your mother would say
if she knew.
It made me wonder

if Mrs. Schickelgruber wasn't probably
a bit like my grandmother, naive
sincerely bewildered. I imagined her
sitting down with her son

in the Reichstag commissary for lunch.
Dolphie, she would say, We are
all so proud of you.
A modest blush on his face,

she asks, So what
are you doing now?
Killing the Jews, he replies,
and the forkful of salad

freezes in the air,
halfway to her mouth.
Why, she asks.
Because they are evil, he says.

Oh, she says
chewing the lettuce.
In that case,
go ahead.

30 Geese on the Lawn

I am staying in a cottage on Whitefish Lake.
In front is a vast green lawn
with a gradual slope
down to the seawall.

On the lawn at the water's edge
are 30 large Canadian Geese
eating seed and hunting through the grass.
There is a commotion and loud honking

as the largest male flies in
and scatters the flock.
I walk down to have a closer look,
hoping that one of them will leave a feather.

There is goose shit everywhere, in the grass
and covering the top of the seawall.
The large male is strutting among the flock
and whenever another male comes close, he

rushes at him hissing and flapping his wings.
Then he puffs out his chest, rises up
and struts about in his own shit.
It still amazes me that humans think

they are so different
from the other creatures.

Getting Famous

Young men and women do not be fooled
by the dealers in dreams.
They would have you believe
that if only your work gets seen
by the right person, somehow
fame will shower you.
It's a trick, a con; everyone
is drowning, no one is special, no one
knows how the Light works or
why it is suddenly on them.
Give no thought to fame,
you are being taken in by lies,
seduced by the promise of order
just beneath the surface and
if you just make the right moves then
you will fit in, you will be
one of them
who is loved by the millions.
There is no love in fame;
it drains you dry and then it
spits your carcass into a ditch.
There is no order to fame, it is
chaos, 3 people waiting for a bus
and a car out of control
strikes the middle one.
You can't outsmart it. If it wants you
it will find you wherever you are
and if it doesn't then
even if you step in front of it, still
it will strike the person in the middle
and leave you standing there
waiting for the bus.

PART II
Death By Surrender

The Way is Within

Alexander of Macedonia was
a very young man when
he conquered what was for him
all of the known world,

all of it.
So his dying words
are instructive:

I should have looked
elsewhere.

The House of a Strong Woman

Suppose Jesus, who was Master,
gave His disciples a task because
He knew He was about to die;

suppose He said to them,
Write down what you have
understood me to be saying.

Thomas the Doubter went off alone.
He simply wrote down word for word
all that he heard from his dear Master's mouth.

And Thomas writes that
this is what Jesus
taught them about women:

And Jesus said to them,
Blessed is the solitary woman...she knows
just where the thieves will enter;

her house may not be ransacked by force,
but if you bind your hands then
all that she has may be easily taken.

Because I am a bit slow like Thomas
I don't understand what Jesus meant
at all, but just suppose He meant

that a man should bow down
and kiss the bare feet of women and
wash them with his tears and dry them

with his hair and only in this way
could he enter the Peaceable Kingdom;
just suppose that is what Jesus meant:

what would you do then?

The Stonecutter and the Potter

He works with marble, she with clay
and that difference is in their marriage like
the darkness of night and the bright day.

His is the rude muscular grace,
the hammer and chisel breaking the stone
to free the angel's face;

hers is the soft consent, thumb and finger
coaxing wet clay into round curve, urged
by the Soul's intent to shape and linger

over the infinite detail. And then he left her,
in the middle of their lives moved downhill
to the cabin he built for his father.

Now there is a coldness like stone
between them. Something is broken
that will not mend like bone

but is ruined, like a good pot
dashed against marble. The fire
which makes clay strong is hot,

the chisel which shapes marble, cold.
The hard angle must give way to the moist curve
or the delicate shape cannot hold.

4 Beautiful Women Approaching Darkness

We are 6 old friends eating Christmas dinner
the way we have so many times before, only
now there is something missing
among the women: 2 of the 4
have just lost ovaries and uterus
to the knife and they are

deeply hurt.
The women speak in low tones
about what it feels like to live in pain
and see the body's delicate line give way,
swell and thicken,
weaken and decay.

The soft voice they use with one another
soothes and adores, it comes from a place
deep within the inner forest,
it is the Soul mourning the body's fate:
they who can no longer bear children
bear their dying with a comely grace

that makes a light shine in the face
and a radiance descends upon them there.
What the body loses in its dying light
the Soul uses to take flight;
while the flesh withers in dark despair,
the Soul grows brilliant in the fading air.

The Fragrance of My Love is Like a Flower
(for Chandrika)

She comes from her bath into my arms,
her scent like rose blossoms in a breeze.
So fresh and delicate are her charms
that I am dizzy and go to my knees,

bend to touch her slippered feet with my lips,
worship and adore her in repose
like a bee drunk among flowers. She slips
one silken slipper and I kiss her toes.

Her skin is soft and sweet
like the petals of a rose. She rises
and her fragrance hovers in retreat,
remains in the room and hours later surprises.

And when for a long time we are apart
it is her scent which lingers in my heart.

The Power of Longing

We forget how deep our longing; we so seldom meet
that our love is a veiled whisper, our passion is discreet.
And then we see each other. What was a smolder
now torches the Heart; it consumes us when I hold her,

leaps between us at the slightest touch.
The smallest kiss is too much
so we refrain.
There are others; we consider their pain

if we are not faithful to our vows.
Restraint in passion can arouse
something so much higher
that the Soul catches fire.

It is often asked what makes a Saint:
I say wild passion, coupled with mild restraint.

Shunyata: Emptiness is Your Friend
(for Little Bear)

I am sitting beneath the Sycamore
next to Snake Creek.
Brown Trout float above brown stones,
a little wind shakes the leaves overhead,
Sunlight falls upon the large boulders,
birdcalls fill the air and
a thin whisper of smoke from our fire
breathes out across the running water.

Emptiness is everywhere
filling the spaces between thinking
the way Sunlight is steadily sinking
into a pool of thin air,

filling what is not there
with a Light that is aware and unblinking.

The King of the World

In Tiruvannamalai, India there is a little beggar
who lived on a garbage heap for 25 years
before He was found out
and they started coming by the thousands
to worship Him. The King of the World
is always a Master of disguise. One

never spoke for 30 years, another
carried bon-bons in His pocket and gave them
to children, held court in whorehouses
and sleazy little Paris dives, but
Yogi Ramsuratkumar lived on the
town garbage dump for 25 years.

They help hold the worlds in balance
and they work in very ordinary ways to do it.
One day 6 disciples
arrived at His house for tea.
He stood there looking at the 6,
walking around and around them.

Then He sat them
in a very precise configuration, placing their cups
exactly, with great care. One of them
moved his cup just a little, and the Yogi
grew instantly alert and severe. This beggar,
He said, Put that cup there for a purpose, and

He knew just what He was doing.
Then He moved it back.
He walked around and around the odd circle,
holding up His staff, stroking His beard, looking
fierce and deeply concentrated, like a King
positioning His armies for an assault.

When He was done and the tea was cold,
He served it. Well,
He said, this beggar did
what He could.
And that is how the King
works to keep the Worlds in line.

In Praise of the Man of Faith

A friend of mine asked the Guru straight out,
How do I get what you've got?
Obedience, devotion,
faith,
surrender, praise,
He replied.

I can do very little of it but
faith and surrender slay me
and faith is the worst because
surrender is just the act of faith.
I got no faith.
I do not trust what I cannot see

and faith is the triumph
of feeling over seeing.
So that is where the Guru comes in.
Mister Lee is faith materialized;
He worships His Father
openly and without guile

so that a sorry little loser like me
can see what faith looks like.
In the absence of faith,
devotion will do.
Mister Lee is devoted to His Father.
I got no devotion.

My heart is small
and broken with fear.
In the absence of devotion,
praise will do
so this poem is praise
from the man who acts alone with no faith

for the man who acts with faith alone.
I bow down to Mister Lee
and praise His noble Heart.
It is all I can do,
a drop of devotion
in an ocean of shame,

a tiny desperate seed of faith
sewn in a desert of doubt.

Why I Am Not Famous

A terrible thing has happened to me:
I have fallen in Love with a Spiritual Master,
the worst thing that could ever happen
to a man like me.
I love fame, adulation, recognition,
notoriety, privilege, honors and awards
but I publish with this invisible little press
known only to a handful of mad disciples,
ignored by critics, media, arbiters of taste
and professors of poetry the world over,
because it is the Guru's press
and I Love the Guru more than recognition,
barely.
So I write for an audience of One
and would rather please that One
than win the adulation of one million;
nothing in this world pleases me so much
as pleasing that One with a poem
I have written.
There is no money in it, the press cannot even
pay to enter my books for the awards,
they cannot advertise, no one knows
I have written another book. Fame
does not come like that, and still
if that One likes what I have written
and sticks it in His journal which goes to
a few hundred disciples scattered here and there
my Heart is full, it is a triumph quite unlike
publishing in the famous journals and
making a name for myself.
Writing for an audience of One
is the greatest thing I've ever done.
I am lost, I am ruined. Oh God
what have You done to me.
My dreams are destroyed;
God help me,
I cannot resist
this anonimity.

Mister Lee and the Art of Flower Arranging

One night during Darshan with Mister Lee,
a disciple gave the Spiritual Master a rose.
Mister Lee broke off the head of the rose
and with great energy flung it

across the Darshan hall toward the large photo
of His own Guru, Yogi Ramsuratkumar,
which was hanging over a small shrine
with a burning candle on it.

The rose landed with a loud THUMP
exactly in the center of the photo
and then fell just next to,
not on top of, not nearby but

just next to
the burning candle and
the flower mala around the photo broke
from the impact of the rose

and fell at the foot of the shrine.

Jesus Lives in Arizona

As usual He was born Jewish
but not to a virgin this time;
that had to go, it was just
too much for people to handle.

He looks the same as always but
this time He has a rock and roll band
and He sings the blues. Jesus would.
He can fool you

if you don't know what to look for because
the holes in His hands and feet are gone
but He still performs the miracles.
One time I went to visit Him and when

I stepped out His door into the overcast day,
instantly the Sun broke through clouds
and as I stood there bathed in a bolt of light
2 Hawks flew right over me, circled and lifted,

drifted out of sight.
Another time He asked me to read a poem
called 'Wolf' and the moment I said the title
His Malamute down by the stable

let out a terrific howl and everyone in the room
fell over laughing and slapping each other's backs.
It will be harder for them to nail Him this time;
He moves around a lot, and His Father is

a street wise old beggar from India
who knows how to work the Trade
better than a carpenter. Jesus is
no fool; one bad trip was enough.

Purna's Teaching

"Train yourself.
Become
a servant of life, do
whatever's needed;
Your life is
not your business:

no thought,
no reflection,
no analysis,
no cultivation,
no intention;

let it
settle
itself."

Naboni's Smoking Mixture

The most famous Baul Master of His time
was Naboni Das Khepa, a Guru of great power
who often meditated at the bottom of a pond
and remained there for a very long time.
But it is Naboni's exceptional capacity
for intoxication
that really reveals His level of attainment.
Anyone can take drugs, smoke, drink to intoxication,
there is nothing unusual in that.
But when a Spiritual Master does these things,
he does it in great quantity and potency
yet remains utterly unaffected by it.
It is said there is a blessing force in it.
Naboni smoked
but ordinary tobacco and even ganja
were not potent enough for Him, so
He mixed tobacco and ganja with jimson weed
soaked in Cobra venom,
put it in a little clay pipe
and happily puffed away on it
as He answered His disciples' questions.
Once one of His senior disciples,
thinking he was able to handle anything
his Master threw at him after so many years of practice,
asked if he could smoke with Naboni.

Sure, He said and handed him the pipe.

The disciple took one small hit,
dropped the pipe, clutched his breast,
began coughing violently and fell over,
his body shaking, his face
turning blue.
Naboni leaned over and blew smoke into his face
at which point the disciple opened his eyes
and his body stopped jerking.

It took him 2 months to recover and it is said
he was never the same again,
that he grew very, very quiet
and no longer showed the slightest trace
of his former arrogance.
No one ever asked
to smoke with Naboni again.

Today You Must Slap Me

It is so easy for me to bullshit myself
in the presence of the Spiritual Master,
believing I know what is going on.
Today Mister Lee told us that
when His Master Yogi Ram laughed,
everyone laughed with Him but
when He laughs we complain,
find fault, turn on Him.

It must be me, He says. I am not doing it
with the innocence of my own Master and
I want you to help me to stop it.
You please stop me every time it happens,
He says and I cannot bear to think
of doing it even once; the pain
of correcting my Master is unbearable;
it breaks my Heart.

One day Meher Baba, who had borne for years
the complaining of His disciples
without a word,
said to them,
Today every time you pass me
you must slap me.
You cannot imagine their horror
but a few did it. The next day

Meher Baba instructed them,
Today every time you pass me
you must spit on me.
Those few who did it were
utterly transformed;
the power of their humility was so great
that upon first meeting them
one was compelled to bow down.

The Argument for Whipping Our Children
(for Monty Roberts)

Old Man Roberts was a violent, brutal man,
for 40 years a trainer of horses.
He did it the way it had always been done,
with whips, ropes, chains and clubs.

This was called 'sacking out' and it
usually took 3-4 weeks
to beat a green horse into submission.
Then his young son Monty came along,

a boy who loved horses and spent his childhood
closely observing them the way a lover
learns the every move and tongue
of his beloved's fleshy speech.

And he began to train his horses
in a way that enraged his father.
His method is simple:
he walks into a round 50 foot pen

as the green horse enters without halter or rope;
he has no whip, chain or spur, nothing
at all in his hands;
first the horse runs, then

it makes eye contact, cocks the ear
nearest to Monty, begins to salivate and lick
as its mouth softens and chews; finally
it lowers its head

and comes close to the Human who
stands easily alone in the center of the ring.
The horse enters willingly into the process
which Monty calls the 'join up'.

Within 30 minutes
of the horse's entry into the pen
it is saddled, bridled and easily ridden.
One day Monty went to his father

and showed the Old Man his method.
Old Man Roberts flew into a rage.
He grabbed a 4-foot stall chain and
beat Monty until he was hospitalized.

Monty changed the world of horse training
with his simple, gentle way.
One old horse trainer
spoke of Monty:

20 years from now
everyone will use his way.
We've got to;
it's the right thing, he said.

The Last Time I Hit My Daughter

Little Wind was 5
and I was a broken man
ruined by divorce and barely alive
in one tiny room of a boarding house,

hating what I had become.
One day I swatted Little Wind on her belly
and ordered her into the hall; dumb
with old sorrows, I closed the door.

Horror instantly vanquished rage.
I opened the door and she stood there
straight and unflinching; old in her age,
she was the noblest human being I ever saw.

On my knees there my life changed, ceased
falling, raised good bread from damaged yeast.

Humbled By Love

You say you had a father once
and though you wished he were a prince
he turned out to be a shameful dunce,
a hopeless idiot bereft of common sense

whose behavior would shame a wild boar?
Well I am one like that, a man whose fear
wounded my daughters. Men like me adore
our children, though we tremble at our

ignorance, are foolish and without grace
in our devotion. But slowly what is gross
in us gives way to the child's fearless embrace
the way a barren plain yields to lush grass.

Though in his arrogance the proud man stumbles,
worship of his child ennobles as it humbles.

My Daughter's First Smile

All of my life I searched in vain
for the woman whose smile was just for me,
whose face lit and creased with ecstacy
when I walked in the room, whose Heart

broke wide open at the sight of me
and who could not stop smiling in delight
when I held her gently in the night.
The only place I never thought to look

was in the face of a child, so when
my daughter was born, life had not prepared
me for the thunderous shock of Love which ensnared
my Heart at once and made me its lifelong,

willing, happy and obedient slave.
For weeks after her birth I gazed
in utter devotion and dumbfounded, amazed
ignorance at her watchful, intelligent face

but I could not in all of my life imagine
the feeling when she looked at me and smiled.
My Heart broke wide open for this small child
who plainly and without reservation adored me.

I stood there lost and ruined, struck dumb,
thinking: At last, dear God at last, she has come.

The Placental Broth

The Indians made a broth
of the placenta and
the mother drank the brew.
They said it made her uterus draw up
and back in place in 3 or 4 days
and I have seen it work that way.
Here is how they did it:

they caught an old range-fed hen
and simmered it on a low fire
for 2 hours in 3 quarts of spring water.

With it they threw in
one big handful of cut celery,
another of carrots and
3 whole scallions with a pinch of salt.

Now here are the 2 secret herbs
which they had on hand but
you will have to hunt them up:
4 slices Wombroot (Dong Qui),
8 slices Milkvetch (Huang Qi).

Strain the broth.
Wash and clean the placenta well
and simmer it in the stock 45 minutes
then strain the broth again.

Drink one pint 2 times a day
for 3 days after delivery.
This is how the woman takes back
her spirit and mends the hole
the child leaves in her power.

Then her milk will have power
and so will she;
she can raise her child straight and true,
she can lend a strong hand,
she can make her stand.

The Gift of the Parents

My child, before you thank me for your life,
beware. The gift is a 2-edged sword.
On one hand you'll be daughter, mother, wife,
and on the other, Death is now your Lord.

It is a gift to be of Humans born,
but we're 2 natures, a truth and a lie;
what's true in us is calm, what's false is torn
by the fact that we all are born to die.

Your gratitude is good, but see it right:
Life rises from Soul's longing for the chance
to make a world, in union both with Light
and with its consort, The Lord of the Dance;

remember love that those who gave you breath,
gave you as well its dancing shadow, Death.

The Impossible Elegance of Power

My first boss in the university
was a woman. She fired a man,
hired me to replace him.
8 months later when I arrived,
she was gone, ousted by friends
of the man she fired.

They were in charge now and
the first thing they did when I got there
was rehire their friend.
5 years later I came up for tenure,
walked in to meet with the tenure committee,
and the man she fired

was the head of my committee.
18 years I try for another job.
No one will touch me and
the woman who hired me, the only one
who can tell my story truthfully,
is retired,

teaches an occasional class
but never in the summer
and never in the English Department.
The summer of my 18th year in exile
a college finally shows some interest,
but the dean who is hiring

takes one look at my resume and sees
6-years-and-out at the last place I taught, so
he makes a blind cold call, praying
there is someone still around
who can tell my story.
One day that very summer

the woman who hired me
drops by the English office, where
she still has a mailbox,
to pick up her summer mail.
The secretary has to pee,
asks if she will mind the phones

for just a moment.
Sure,
she says.
The secretary steps
out of the office and
the phone rings.

Robert E. Lee in Richmond

It was after the war, well after
the awful crushing burden of defeat
had time to sink deeply in.
Lee was revered in Richmond because

he showed others grace in suffering
which helped them to find their own way
through the terrible wound of their
sorrows.

Lee found himself one day in church
about to take communion when
a black man walked to the front
and the entire congregation froze.

Though all eyes did not turn to Lee,
in that long momentary silence
everyone was aware of his presence
and did not know what to do.

Lee arose at once and
without hesitation went to the front,
knelt there
alongside the man, and

took communion with him.
Though others make a case for Chancellorsville,
I argue that this moment
was Lee's greatest triumph.

Jimmy Driftwood's Guitar
(for BR)

They were dirt poor country people.
When they moved to Tennessee in a wagon
his grandmother brought her cherry wedding bed,

a kitchen table and 2 chairs.
His grandfather brought farm tools and an ox yoke.
But the music would not let him alone

and when he could be quiet no longer,
he used what was at hand to make the guitar:
she gave him her cherry bed rail

and he made the neck from it,
used the ox yoke for the sides,
top and bottom were from her headboard.

There is a love that humans sometimes come to,
which gives everything for beauty
and gladly sleeps on a hard floor

so a young boy they only dreamt of
can pick up the strung ox yoke,
pluck it like a farmer snapping reins

and while the grand ghosts dance he
makes their cherry wedding bed
sing.

Mike Disfarmer, Shadow-Seer

He lived in Heber Springs, Arkansas
next to the post office. He claimed
that a tornado picked him off the ground
in Germany and landed him in a potato row
in Arkansas. He was the
only photographer in town, by all accounts
grouchy, eccentric, and most important
absolutely not interested in posing them
so they posed themselves: farm people
worn by their common labor,
in love with the dirt and one another so
they stand together and they do not smile
because dirt does not reward the artful pose.
In 1959 they found Disfarmer dead a week
on the floor in his seedy studio.
A lawyer from Little Rock bought his
photographic plates, thousands of them,
for 5 dollars and they have
made Disfarmer famous, finally.
So much for the actual value of fame,
but the real Art is not a thing of this world,
it is a Mystery and we serve it.
It may finger an old recluse
in a bad mood, but once the Light descends
they cannot help themselves:
in bib overalls, aprons and blue jeans
they walk through the dirt fields,
their burned faces etched like wormwood,
and they stand there
in the cramped musty dinge of his studio,
shadows on their brow like a deathhand
and the old man hunched with sorrows
comes out from the back room;
without words he gestures to the
hard wooden benches or the cracked blank wall
and they arrange themselves in their history;
he throws the black cloth over his head

and disappears into the real Art, scowling
through a glass darkly into the shadows, waiting
for the moment when the world
ceases to grind and
the Light appears for a moment before
the little men and women of the Earth
sink once again
beneath the shadows.

2 Ways of Crossing the Creek

Just this side of the reservation
over Big Rapids Creek,
there is a fine bridge built by
the CCC in the thirties.
You know the kind:
careful work of proud men
who were ruined by the times.
Stone and wood it was
a pretty thing and
heavily used by the traffic.

Half-a-mile down in the woods
I come across 6 Indian men
who have felled and trimmed
a big tree and are tying ropes
around its 2 remaining limbs
which they throw to one who
stands on the other side.
Then they all walk the
half-mile to the bridge,
cross over and down to where
the man with the ropes waits.

I sit there and watch, even push
and tug at the limbs as they
strain and heave the tree
across the rapid creek, then
after 2 hours of sweat they
walk across it, big smiles
all over their bronze faces.

I ask them,
why go to all this trouble
when there's a fine bridge near?

They look at me curiously
and hand me a beer.
They shake their heads and
laugh but do not speak,
as if a man who needs to ask
is already too far gone, as
if he is the kind of man who
would build a bridge when
a log would do.

The Digger of Shallow Wells
(Shallow Well Project: 618-997-5365)

Tom Logan is my oldest friend.
When we were boys he was the one
with a vision. I just followed along,
glad to be in his company.
We ran with Blacks, 2 white boys
in a hard crowd
on the dark side of town.
Now Tom spends 1/2 his time in Africa
digging shallow wells. Some job
for a visionary, you might say.

But I would tell you that real visions
are simple and save lives.
In Africa 15,000 children die every day,
mostly from diarrhea
because of bad water.
In 3 years Tom and his people dug
84 shallow wells at a cost of $300 each
so 25,000 people had safe drinking water.
The children no longer
shit themselves to death.

This is how a man with a vision works:
he goes up the filthy Lukulu River and he
finds a spot where villagers drink from
an open hole in the stream;
he digs, the villagers put in pipe,
stones, cement, pump; the children dance
and sing and drink with cupped hands.
They no longer shit themselves to death.

Logan is trapped, just like you and me,
but his is the trap of angels,
a man snared by a vision, ruined by
the light so he must dig
or die. Such a man will
die like the rest of us, may
amount to nothing in the meantime, but
he will not be one who
shits himself to death
like you and me.

How the Drought Behaves

The Drought walks about
and views the water supplies.
He is feverish and driven with thirst,
full of pity

at the sighing of the dying wells
deep down as they are drying and
giving up what remains of their wet souls
to the bottom slime and impure mud.

Imagine His joy when He finds
there is still a small seepage
from the farmer's spring, like blood
from a moist wound.

He finds no pleasure at the village wells
where nothing grows but people's thirst
and even the dugs of the women
are shriveled and dry,

their children gaunt and hollow of eye.
Tell us a story, they cry and tug at Him
so He sits on the curb by the dry well
and gathers the shy children in His arms.

He tells them the history of each
well, spring, stream and river
which ever existed in that country
and what became of them.

Their laugh is exhausted, like a dry cough.
He rises to go but they will not let Him.
Tell us of the morning dew, how fat drops
gathered on each leaf and gleaming stalk

they beg Him and He does, adding
for their pleasure the histories of
snow melt, flood, cactii and roots
that you could slice open and drink.

Oh how the children of the thirst
love Him and weep when He departs
but He has to go.
He has heard of a well in the mountains

which still holds its water-mirror
shining very near to the opening and
stars are still reflected in the dark.
He goes there and sits patiently,

never forsaking it until drop by drop
it dies out, the thistles shrink,
the grass yellows and rasps
and rattles in the hot dry wind

like the last breath of a man
long suffering and acquainted with thirst.
The Drought rests then
by the Perpetual Well where

the angels of water care for Him,
give Him good drink for His thirst
and wrap His fever in cool wet rags
until men forget Him again and take

abundance as their right and privilege.
Then He rises and goes sorrowing among them,
everywhere viewing the water supplies
and priming the wellsprings of compassion.

The Long Legged Heron in the Water

She is dead one year today.
The frail birch canoe is light and easy
among the reeds in the dark troubled waters,
the hint of approaching storm

stirring their depths the way a woman,
awaiting her lover's touch,
feels her belly heave restlessly.
In the weedy shallows the turtles rise

and climb upon the old logs;
I float among the hollow reeds, birch
rasping against cane, the clouds
hovering above the water like a lover

poised to press his body into her flesh.
The wind shakes the reeds raggedly
like the breath of a woman near orgasm,
or the same woman in my arms

in a darkened room, same breath,
approaching death. The Blue Heron
comes in low and circling, soundless
and queenly against the gathering storm.

She lands in the shallows, pulls one leg
softly from the water the way the Soul
lifts easily without sound from the
troubled beauty of a woman's body or

her lover pulls reluctantly away
from union; exhausted with love
and the frustrations of the body he
dips and feathers, pulls out

into the lake heading for home.
Behind him the hollow reeds quiver
and brush in the wind, the Blue Heron
grows distant, then invisible

in the slowly descending darkness.

The Beautiful Poem Written By A Tree

It lasts only for a season
and then for a good reason
it is gone
and only a bird song
remains,
singing Her endless refrains.

Her limbs rhyme with the sky and
Her leaves with the high wind,
Her fruit with the shy hand,
Her roots with the dry land.

Her meter
slows as her aging fruit grows sweeter.
No living thing may cheat Her
lest it come to grief beneath Her.

PART III
Death By Attention

For Vedan, Who Died Young

She had such good luck:
she didn't have to watch her body
waste away from around her,
or see her looks run away
and leave her with a face
like a badly used burlap bag;

she didn't have to stand accused by her children
after they had lost all their innocence;
she never had to give up on romantic love.

And in that instant
when they all knew the plane was finished
and they still had one breath left in their allotment
maybe she remembered
that she had lived with a Master
who taught her to be a Watcher,
a passer-by.

And in that superb moment
as the body was rent by impact and flame
maybe, because she had such good luck,
she stayed quiet and still
and shot out of the used up body
like a poised stone from a sling,

right into the waiting arms
of her Guardian
who flew with her to the highest point
where she was allowed the one last dance
due those who leave with attention
and she danced like a woman gone mad
because she had nothing left to lose.

Maybe.
Because she had such good luck.

Voluntary Simplicity

It is like the woman waking early in the farmhouse
with her lover dead beside her in the bed.
She is alone
and the one thing that matters most is gone.

She drags and carries his naked body to the barn,
heaves it over the field horse's broad back,
and stands there naked except for her boots.
Shovel in hand she clambers up behind him

and heads for the orchard in a stately prance.
Her breasts dance
in a slow undulant of woe
and she does not care who sees
as she moves along the fence row
toward the sweet apple trees.

In a mist of tender fury
she boots a hole root deep
and plants her man
so his taste will season the crop
and his rot will feed the twist
of appleroot.

Then it is over and she lies
face down in the dust.

Later, in a slow and patient heap
she drags and stacks his furniture in the yard,
his shirts, books, everything.
Death sweeps clean.
She lights and blazes it heavenward.

The rooms are nearly empty now
and so is she.
Like a green and tender tree
she prunes her sorrow.

Finally, in her hot bath, she weeps.

The Law of Karma

We know nothing of this world and
we have lost our sense of wonder but
there is more going on here than we can
possibly imagine with our scientific minds.

Take the disciple of the Zen Master who
made a serious mistake and
to work off the karma from this act
his Master gave him the penance

of incarnating as a fox
over and over again for 500 years.
500 years later a Zen Master and His disciples
notice that a fox comes and sits

in the trees at the edge of the clearing
every time the Master gives a talk.
The fox sits straight and attentive,
taking in every word and when it is over

he disappears into the woods.
This goes on for many years until one day
the disciples find the fox's body
dead in the woods.

They take it to the Master who tells them
they must bury it with great care
and pray for it as this fox is
one of them and

will soon be coming back in human form.
We are ignorant people;
we know nothing of our lives
and take no care for our actions

or our words, thinking
we only pay if we are caught.
With our scientific minds we think
the fox sitting at the edge of the clearing

is just a fox, nothing more.

The Boy Jesus in the Wood Shop

The air was heavy with the scent of shavings
and the sweat of men working with wood.
The apprentices had one corner where they
planed and did the rough cuts.

This is where He stayed mostly, fetching
lumber and cleaning tools but now and then
His father called Him over so He could feel
the grain of a smooth piece, how the gnarls

and bolls twisted like the river of love
through the sullen breast and how the carpenter
smoothed and worked the wood, how he
shaped and fitted, made holes and pegs

to fill the holes, tongues and grooves
to receive them and it made His heart glad.
One day He dropped something and it broke.
His father raised his hand to cuff Him

but Jesus stood straight and firm.
No father, He said and Joseph's hand
froze in air, then fell to his side.
All work stopped, man and boy, as they

watched Joseph go to one knee and hold his Son.
Then it started up again but they were troubled,
each one of them secretly wondering
why he had never thought to stand up

to his own father
and what it took to do it
that they were missing and
could not find or even name.

God is in the Details

Most of the farms now are factories,
but not Jake Miller's.
He is one of the last small farmers in the county,
plows with 2 horses,
farms 30 acres, grows
corn, beans, vegetables
and a little smoke in the woods.
But what I want to talk about mainly
is his tool box
and his plow.
Jake's tool box is polished wood,
small, neat and simple,
mounted between the handles of the plow.
There are 4 tools in it:
pliers, screwdriver, wrench, putty knife.
With them he can fix anything
that goes wrong.
The plow is 60 years old,
belonged to his father.
Each night with the
wrench and screwdriver
he checks the nuts and bolts,
tightens,
scrapes the mud from it
with the putty knife,
wipes it down,
oils the wood until
the plow shines,
hangs it up on its hooks,
retires for the night:
a religious man.

The Good Farmer

Jake Miller is an old style farmer,
still plows with horses,
herds his cattle on foot.
He hired 2 young farm hands to help him,

senior Ag majors from the local college,
and they got in trouble
driving some wild cattle with sticks
on horseback. They had never seen

anything like Jake in their classes.
When he saw they were in trouble
he called them off and walked out
into the small herd,

hands in his pockets,
speaking softly to the cattle the way
a good father soothes frightened children.
He walked slowly beside them

and they followed along like
obedient children, softly lowing.
You never pressure an animal
from the rear, he told them.

They're just like people.
They don't like to be chased;
if you want to really get someone upset
just follow around close behind them, he said.

For a few the field is as Sacred
as the Temple, the cow
equal to the Lord. These
are the few who grow Holy.

The cows gather about him in the field,
their wide wet nostrils inhale him,
their rough tongues lick his hands,
they worship what they know to be true.

Spiritual Practice is Not Complicated

It is said that John Coltrane
would get in a groove
while playing and
sometimes would play for hours
and hours and he
could not stop.

Once he talked to Miles Davis
about this because it was
becoming a problem for his band.
I get going and I can't stop,
he told Miles.
Simple, man

Miles said,
smiling.
You just
take the horn
out of your
mouth.

Mosquito Hawk

I am sitting deep in the forest by Snake Creek
early in the morning, quietly watching
when a tall blade of grass on the opposite cliff
catches my eye. There is no wind but
it is bobbing and weaving, bending like
the pole of a fisherman with something big
on the end of its line.
It is a Mosquito Hawk snagged on a spider's line;
it has broken one end but cannot get free of the other
and now it is doing its last aerial dance,

a fearful, frantic frenzy, everything in it
focused, every ounce of it
intent on breaking free
but it is no good,
it spins in wild circles round and round and
this goes on for a long time until it drops,
exhausted and
the tiny spider starts slowly down the line.

For a moment I consider freeing fellow Hawk but
just then at my feet where I am crouched by the creek
a Copperhead comes swimming downstream and I see
it is no use.
You break free of one line and there is another
waiting for you.

A small black fly lands on my leg;
I brush it off and it drops to the ground;
one wing hopelessly damaged,
it crawls off.

The Arrowsmith Woman

Her work is wood, stone, and feather
notched in a passionate symmetry like
a gentle man entering a virtuous woman.
She holds the shaft softly in her hand,

straight Hickory branch, cuts it
with a graceful regret, the way
a woman cuts her chord
to set the baby free.

She strips and notches it,
shaves it round and round
between thumb and finger until
the balance is perfectly right;

like 2 lovers who live apart, the art
is to find the exact midpoint
between longing and lingering, then
to pause there as the shaft is poised

on one finger, her life
in the balance. She quarries stone
in small blocks, cradles them like
lifting a newborn to her breast.

Then the careful chip and flute,
notches and nestles stone in shaft,
wraps with tendon, tightly ties.
She lifts feather from stilled wing,

Jay, Redbird, Finch,
all fly true in the heart
of wood where feather
complements stone.

Then she hands her life over
to the hunters like a woman gives her child
to the world in delicate consent,
having done all the things

which are possible to make it
perfectly true to its aim,
able to give beautifully and
to take terribly away.

The Medicine Stone

Begin with a river or a stream.
Stand by it a long time watching,
then in it looking and
you can find a good stone.

It must suit you the way
a good woman's body suits you when
you are lying naked together, touching and her
warm roundness is perfectly fitted

against your hard angles: like that
as it lies in the palm of your hand.
For me that means a round smoothness
just like that woman Chandrika

is round and smooth, weathered and shaped
by the river of time running ceaselessly
over and around her flesh.
Then you take this river stone and

you find a small bag perfectly suited for it,
one whose size and shape fit
just right
as Chandrika fits my body;

stone and bag must please eye and hand
the way Chandrika soothes my seeing
and completely fulfills the longing
of my palm and fingertips.

If you carry this stone in its bag
like a fertile egg in its uterine sack,
and you hold it when there's a need,
it can begin subtle changes in you friend

which arouse the sleeping woman
dozing in your fleshy male dream.
I am not speaking of a sexual thing
but of a feeling long hidden and in deep

for the Earth and its creatures, a feeling
like a naked mother has when she
gives the nipple to her child, a thing
men do not want to feel because

they can never be the same again.
You hold the stone in your hand
the way a woman holds the child's head
and you let the Medicine work your body,

but be sure you want to disappear friend
because that is where this goes: you
disappear and
something else stands in your place;

begin with a river or a stream.

The Courage of Sitting Bull

I am reading in the paper about
the gang-boys and how they
shoot people from moving cars
to prove their bravery. This

reminds me of Sitting Bull, who
went in 1872 to fight the army on Elk River
with Crazy Horse and hundreds of warriors.
At daybreak the soldiers were lined up

in thickets and behind the river bank
when Sitting Bull strolled out onto the open meadow
within plain sight of the soldier lines.
He carried his fringed pipe bag and tobacco pouch.

"Who other Indians wish to smoke with me,"
he shouted at his warriors, and he sat down.
As he calmly filled the bowl with tobacco,
4 warriors came cautiously to sit by their Chief.

Each puffed vigorously and passed the pipe quickly
around the circle. Sitting Bull never spoke. He
looked around calmly and smoked long and quietly
as bullets kicked up dirt and sang past his head.

When the bowl was empty, he cleaned it as the
others ran back to cover. Then he rose, put the
pipe in its bag and slowly turned his back on
the enemy fire, walking calmly into the brush.

Once young boys knew what courage was;
they saw it in their leaders,
not courage to kill someone
which many have,

but courage to die
which has always been
in short supply.

Sitting Bull's Revenge

By 1887, even Sitting Bull had given up
his rifle and his horse and was held
prisoner of war at Standing Rock, the last
of the Sioux to go down.

Few still believed in Sitting Bull's powers.
Many of the captives quickly forgot the old ways
and adopted the customs of their captors.
Shell King was one of them.

Once an able warrior, he took to farming
and sided with the agent against his Chief.
Sitting Bull called him on it publicly one day.
Enraged, Shell King attacked him with a knife.

Sitting Bull pulled his battle axe but
before either could strike, the tribal police
disarmed them and took the weapons.
Ten days later Shell King was walking the road

near the agency when a big storm hit
without warning. A great black cloud
appeared from nowhere and let loose a brilliant
burst of lightning which struck Shell King,

killed him where he stood.
Not many men can fight like that:
smoke the pipe, call the rain cloud,
let the son of a bitch have it.

Sitting Bull's Horse
(for Little Bear)

Sitting Bull said, A horse is
a Spirit Being who has not forgotten
where he came from, therefore
He is superior to most human beings.

In his old age, Sitting Bull
rode in Cody's Wild West Show
on the same horse he had ridden
since he was a young boy,

an intelligent horse trained to prance
every time the guns volleyed
at the end of the show.
Then Sitting Bull quit the show because

he got involved in Wovoka's Ghost Dance
and he rode his horse to the Dances
and the horse stood and watched
intently.

When the tribal police shot Sitting Bull
for defying agency orders to stop dancing,
every eyewitness reports the same thing:
As the first volley of gunfire

took Sitting Bull down
his horse began to dance and he
danced in a way they had never seen;
on and on he danced while

Sitting Bull died;
2, 3 hours he danced and
no one could catch him or
make him stop.

Some of the Sioux say he was
doing the Ghost Dance for Sitting Bull,
others say it was Sitting Bull's Spirit
showing the people that

you cannot kill a free man.

Grass Dancer

Picture if you can the lean face of Grass Dancer
whose mouth turned down at the corners and
whose gaze was cold and unwavering
no matter the circumstances.
His face paint was always a thin black circle
around each eye
so his gaze fired from this darkness like
a man with a knife
flying at you from out of a tree.
He was a master of the knife
and the Lakota people still tell of Grass Dancer

alone in a tree guarding the horses
when a Crow raiding party came out of the dark,
10 men on foot and horseback
and they were on top of Grass Dancer
before he even had time to shout.
So he killed them all,
all 10 of them with a knife and an axe
and when they found him he was
hurt so bad they thought he
could not live
but he did.

When he was old and nearly dead
the first white writers found him
and one of them asked, What was it like
to kill 10 men single handed.
He gazed at them with mild contempt.
I was guarding the horses, he said.
The people counted on me;
there was no other choice.
In this way real honor arose and then
disappeared slowly from this land
the way a fire flickers in the darkness,

flairs up for a moment brightly
and then goes softly out, leaving
everything unguarded and afraid.

The Namer

Red Hawk was the oldest man I've known.
He came that first time to my vision quest
by the Buffalo River.

He made a big limb fall at my feet;
he made a big dog come to my tent like a pup
and befriend me.
        These are very little things, he said,
just to get the attention of a fool.

Later he made me see what I am
without lies and pretending.
        This is a bigger thing, he said,
getting a fool to pay attention
to himself.

Still later I saw how I am little
and live at the Mercy of something big.
That slowed me down and shut me up.
        This is a big thing, he said,
filling a fool's attention
with Mercy.

        The last time I saw him he said,
You take this name I am wearing.
I'm finished with it.
It is a big name
and you will feel its weight.

It will be a burden and demand
more than a little man can give.
This name will change you.
This is a good name for a little man
        he said.

And he left me with that.

After the Poetry Reading

As I am exiting the hall
a fresh-faced, earnest young man
collars me, one of the
ardent Baptist boys

Arkansas breeds like locusts
in a field of ripe corn.
Mister Hawk, he says sincerely,
Why do you use

so many dirty words?
Like what, I ask honestly surprised.
Shit and
asshole, he replies.

Don't worry about it, son
I say as I go through the door;
Everyone does it,
everyone has one and

everyone is one sometimes.

Some Meditations on the Art of Poetry

Given 2 good choices, both unfettered
in their meaning, the simpler is better.

Mastery of rhyme was understood by Frost:
impossible to say which rhymed word came first;

that rhyme is most sound
which surprises when it's found.

Irony is the rarest quality in verse,
wit next; their absence is a curse.

Brevity is not only the soul of wit,
no virtue in verse overshadows it.

If the queen of virtue is brevity,
her handmaiden is humility.

Who thinks they've found the truth, hesitate
and when they write it down, understate.

If the choice is form or meaning,
form needs weaning.

Real art is hard, but the hardest part is
ars celare artis.

What is seen in great poems as art
is in truth the urgency of the heart.

Those who believe they are the source
sew the seeds of their remorse;

those who serve something higher
step into a holy fire

where they burn.
This is what the best poets learn.

The secret to revision is well known:
cut it to the bone.

The secret to reading well:
risk the whisper, conserve the yell;

let the poem create the spell,
chatter in-between is mostly hell;

keep it shy of an hour,
and mix wit with power,

grief
with comic relief.

"Poems Should Be Written Rarely and Reluctantly . . .
(. . . Czeslaw Milosz)

. . . Under unbearable duress,"
Milosz went on, and did not say
but meant, with no thought of success,
no hope of being understood unless

the threat of jail or being shot
is the truest success a poet could pray
for, the clear recognition that he has not
missed his target. What rot

we get without reluctance;
lacking humility a poet's words betray
him. He misses his best chance
at truth when he does not glance

over his shoulder at death and write
as if his life depended on it. This is the way
of duress: a man speaks only when fright
is outshone by a blinding flash of light

which illuminates a handful of dust
and makes it briefly into a poet, clay
into flesh; and though reluctant, then he must
write poems; uncorrupted by moth or rust.

How Rare to Find Honor Among the Artists

I live in a small state where
the poets know one another and are
seldom generous.
But there are the rare stories
which make a different point, such as
in the Italy of Leonardo's time
there was a famous competition
for the Florence Baptistry doors.
Brunelleschi and Donatello,
2 of the finest artists of their day,
both submitted models for the competition.
Remember, this was in a day when
universities did not succor middling talent;

if you lost a commission, you lost
standing, honor and livelihood.
But when the entries were exhibited
and the 2 artists went to view them
they were stunned by Ghiberti's work
which they saw at once
was superior to their own.
They went to the consuls immediately
and argued that Ghiberti
should get the commission
which he did. And
it is said the 2 men
were happy.

Miller Williams Delivers the Inaugural Poem

He is old and frail, not as far gone
as Frost who read for JFK, but
he has been around and it shows.
He walks out there, one lone poet

armed only with the truth while
the rows of politicians are lined up
behind him, men striving for power
who will do anything, say anything,

kill anyone
to get it.
It is no contest; the poet
is striving to tell the truth

before a massed congregation of liars
and the contrast is remarkable,
no one can miss it, it does not matter
if the poem is any good at all. It is

obvious why poets are so seldom seen
at the affairs of state: the politicians
cannot afford to be seen with men
who are striving to tell the truth.

Politics

The dogs
were electing a president.
One nominated the bulldog;
No good, others wailed.
He can fight but he can't run.

Another nominated the greyhound;
No good, they all wailed.
He can run, but he can't fight.
Then a sorry little mongrel stood up.
I nominate the one who smells sweet

under his tail; that one's honest, he said and
immediately all the dogs' ears raised up.
They all began eagerly sniffing
under each other's tail.
Whew, he's not presidential quality;

Ugh, that's not our boy;
Whoa, he's no president.
And today if you go out in the streets
you can see they are
still trying to sniff out

the rightful candidate.

2 Breeds of Cat

When the old woman next door died
one of her daughters came over to ask me
would I help her take the 2 cats to the vet's
so they could be put to sleep.

Fluffy, the fat male, came easily.
He didn't have a clue.
He climbed up into her arms making noises
like he would never die.

But the other one, Snowball,
the one she needed help with,
knew what was up and she
was not about to go easily.

Backing and hissing, under one piece
of furniture and then the next, finally
she raced for the stairs to the second floor.
I found her under the bed where the

old woman died. When I dove for her
she left deep wounds on both arms, went
through the closed window leaving glass
everywhere, down a tree and into the sewer.

I see her in the neighborhood now and then.
She is lean and feral.
No human can get close to her.
Some of us can be domesticated so

when the time comes to lead us
to the slaughter
we follow without question.
Then there are the others.

What It Takes

The first job I ever had, 15 years old,
was the night desk clerk at the
Saint Nicholas Hotel, with a bar
next to the desk where the whores

and the bums drank.
The whores loved me and they
interested me immensely, but it was
Julian I remember well.

He was a bum and a serious drunk.
The others drank, and heavily, but
they looked around, they talked, they
all had this hope that somehow

things might change for them,
someone might walk in that dark
and sorry place who would make
the difference for them.

Not Julian. He never spoke to anyone,
the rest of them stayed away from him,
he just downed shot after shot and
looked straight ahead. He was

the most single minded man I ever saw,
not aimless and confused like the others,
not hedging his bets. He had real intention
and he never deviated from his aim.

Julian was different from the others;
he had what it takes
to be a success
in this world.

Nothing Left

Nothing interests me anymore.
The days crawl by like
worms after a hard rain and
I can sit here on my screened porch
from dawn until dark, doing nothing
just watching the shadows move
from one tree to the other until
everything is bathed in a pale dark,
like my empty heart.
Sports used to interest me but they have
been completely corrupted by greed
and a brutal disdain for the fans.
The newspaper once held some hope for me
because of the funnies, but no more:
Calvin and his tiger were the last breath
of true madness and common idiocy
left in a waste of the simply stupid.
TV is one crushing bore after another
interspersed with deafening commercials
duller than the worst shows.
I sit here on my screened porch and
all of a sudden here she comes again.
Every day this beautiful woman with
long brown hair nearly to her gorgeous butt
comes walking. Today she has on tight shorts
and her legs are splendidly muscled, the
calves curved and bulging, the thighs
2 tapering pillars of tanned flesh so fine
I can almost feel the hairs with my lips
and then she is gone over the hill.
Where was I? Oh, yes
nothing interests me
anymore.

The Condemned Man

They just killed a con up at Tucker,
a murderer name of Frankie Parker.
He got a lot of publicity, seems
he became something like a
Buddhist monk there on death row.
One of the local Buddhists calls me,
wants me to phone the governor
and plead for Frankie's life.
I decline.

Looks like Frankie has all the luck.
He murdered 2 people so
he has to pay, we all do,
for everything.
But he gets to pay all at once,
not a little at a time for a
very long time like the rest of us.

And he found a spiritual practice which,
if he was sincere in it,
could help him at the moment
of his death
and at the execution there will be those
who would help him remember it.

He has a good chance
to die a Conscious death, quick
and prepared for, not slow, not
lingering in a sterile room,
plugged, tubed and comatose.
So I don't make the call.

I live on death row too,
we all do and
nobody
is making any calls
for me.

Zero the Swine Clerk

Serving 5-to-15 for Murder 2 he has
finally found a place in this world
that suits him: he shoots pigs

on the prison farm, only now he uses a
needle, not the nasty little .38 he used
to murder his girlfriend and when he

shovels shit now it is the swines'
and not the stinking mess that was
what he came to call his life.

He is my friend and I saw him go
all the way with whiskey and pot,
as far as you can go and live, from

man to swine rooting in Human garbage.
But strange things happen; consider this:
by serving the swine, shoveling their shit,

feeding them the garbage slops and
inoculating them against disease,
Zero is uplifted.

He comes to see that humble devotion
is our only life, and a man who
could not love Humans loves the pigs

and carries his remorse the way
a farm boy carries his slops bucket: day
after day he lugs it without complaint

and his burden strengthens him. The pigs
love him, grunt when he appears, forgive
his slightest clumsy stumble.

Zero the Feed Mill Clerk

Things change,
even men, though much more rarely
than you would probably imagine.

They have promoted Zero from
the prison hog farm to the feed mill
where he is the bookkeeper, taking
inventory, filling out requisitions,
typing, balancing the books.
Each morning he makes coffee
for the others, morning and evening
sweeps the office floor.

For a murderer, a dope dealer and
a drunk, this is pretty tame stuff
but I can see he is fulfilled in it.
Shot a woman to death,
dumped her body, left
a trail your mother could follow,
got caught right away.

Now each day, each week, each
month and year he
keeps track of production, accounts
for every last pound of corn,
milo and copper sulfate
that goes to feed the cattle
and the hogs.

After everyone else is gone
into the dark,
Zero stays late to sweep clean,
accounts for what is used up,
balances the books.

For Tom, Whose Baby Died

It is hard for a man
because he does not have the comfort
of hard labor and bodily pain,
of something to be done.

His only solace
is the quiet touch
of his hand on her cheek,
of his eyes humbly sharing with her

an unbearable Love.
He does not give her too much;
his strength comes from the art
of when to look away,

when to remain silent,
when to leave her alone.
He grows by diminishing self.
He serves her in a way

that does not show, that supports
with hidden hand;
and in so doing, he also serves Another
whose heartbeat is a trace

between them, whose breath
he feels on his face
at night
as she turns to softly hold him.

It is a kind of grace
given to a man whose child dies:
that he can humbly labor then,
that he can suffer himself

to bear the heartbeat of his child
and deliver it into the world
as kindness, as service to others,
as humble work done without reward.

Little Wind Learns to Speak

I was young then and still believed
that words were true
and that their mastery
could help unlock the mystery
of the human heart; through
words we could escape the unrelieved

suffering of this life.
So every day I stood with Little Wind in my arms
looking at the trees and repeating
the names of things as if entreating
the Spirit of the World with magic charms
so it would not take its knife

to my daughter's heart.
And every day a dog barked and I said,
Dog.   One day the dog barked
and like a cold engine which is sparked,
she lifted her beautiful innocent head
and said, Gog.   That was the start

of the madness for Little Wind,
the loss of her organic innocence. The word
enters into us and we are lost
to the unspeakable wonder. The cost
of naming is our lives. Like a low flying bird
hit by a car, we do not even know we sinned.

EPILOGUE
We Practice All Our Lives
for a Single Moment

We Practice All Our Lives for a Single Moment

Eric and I are camped deep in the woods.
We are talking about death,
how a whole life of spiritual practice
is for the one single shining moment
when death comes

and destroys the body.
Just as we are talking about this moment
I see a movement in the corner of my eye
on the ground by the tent,
a flutter and a pulsation

like a heart beating;
it is a Luna Moth, a big one,
and it is dying.
There is movement in the wings,
a stifled and hopeless tremor and

then the ants come,
2 big black ones: death comes
for the body which belongs to it.
Soon the Luna is on its back,
its thick white grub-body writhing,

its stubby little white legs flailing
and the ants are tearing it to pieces,
their bodies covered in white moth dust
so they are like ghosts, worker angels
disassembling the great winged-machine.

To be conscious and totally present
at the moment of death
takes a lifetime
of practice
so we do not waver

when the ants come.

About the Author

Red Hawk was the Hodder Fellow at Princeton University. His other books are: *Journey of the Medicine Man* (August House), *The Sioux Dog Dance* (Cleveland State University) nominated for the 1992 Pulitzer Prize in poetry; and *The Way of Power* (Hohm Press) nominated for the 1996 Pulitzer Prize and the 1997 National Book Award. He teaches at the University of Arkansas at Monticello.

Red Hawk is available for readings and lectures/ workshops for an honorarium and travel expenses. He may be contacted at 824 N. Hyatt, Monticello, AR 71655; or via e-mail at: moorer@uamont.edu.